FIRST PEOPLES

THE SAN

OF AFRICA

LINDA J. PARKER

Lerner Publications Company • Minneapolis

**First American edition published in 2002
by Lerner Publications Company**

Published by arrangement with Times Editions
Copyright © 2002 by Times Media Private Limited

Lerner Publications Company
A division of Lerner Publishing Group
241 First Avenue North
Minneapolis, MN 55401 U.S.A.
Website address: www.lernerbooks.com

Series originated and designed by
Times Editions
An imprint of Times Media Private Limited
A member of the Times Publishing Group
1 New Industrial Road, Singapore 536196
Website address: www.timesone.com.sg/te

Series editors: Margaret J. Goldstein, Paul A. Rozario
Series designers: Tuck Loong, Rosie Francis
Series picture researcher: Susan Jane Manuel

Library of Congress Cataloging-in-Publication Data
Parker, Linda (Linda J.)
The San of Africa / by Linda Parker.
p. cm. — (First peoples)
Includes bibliographical references and index.
Summary: Describes the history, culture, modern and traditional
economies, religion, family life, and language of southern
Africa's San people, as well as the region in which they live and
their struggle to maintain cultural traditions in a modern world.
ISBN 0-8225-4177-7 (lib. bdg. : alk. paper)
1. San (African people)—Juvenile literature.
[1. San (African people)] I. Title. II. Series.
DT1058.S36 P27 2002
968'.004961—dc21   2001004653

Printed in Malaysia
Bound in the United States of America

1 2 3 4 5 6—OS—07 06 05 04 03 02

CONTENTS

WHO ARE THE SAN?

In ancient times, the San were the only occupants of southern Africa. They roamed throughout the region, following the animals they hunted. They lived along coastal regions near the Atlantic and Indian oceans. They also lived in the Drakensberg Mountains, on the open grasslands, and in the Kalahari Desert.

In modern times, these areas are part of the southern African countries of Angola, Botswana, Namibia, the Republic of South Africa, Zambia, and Zimbabwe, and the kingdoms of Lesotho and Swaziland. The modern San form only a tiny part of the populations of these countries.

The San have always been a peaceful people. They have lived without polluting or damaging the environment. They have recorded their history by painting on rock walls and telling vivid folklore. Their culture is at least 30,000 years old.

Newcomers to San Lands

Dutch settlers came to southern Africa in the 1600s. They planted crops and built roads and fences. The San could no longer freely hunt and roam the land from coast to coast. Some San moved north toward the Kalahari Desert. Others lived among the Dutch and other European settlers. Some San married people from neighboring African groups. Their customs and words mixed with those of the outsiders and newcomers. The San languages began to disappear.

Modern-Day San

The modern San live alongside many different groups in the countries of southern Africa. Most modern San live in government camps. Some live in wildlife parks, where they work as hunters or guides. Others earn a living by shearing sheep. They travel from farm to farm to find work. A few San still live in the Kalahari Desert, traveling and hunting as their ancestors did.

HOW MANY?

No one knows how many San live in southern Africa. Survival, an organization in the United Kingdom that highlights the problems of the San, states that there are about 90,500 San: 8,000 in Angola; 45,000 in Botswana; 33,000 in Namibia; 2,500 in the Republic of South Africa; 1,500 in Zambia; and 500 in Zimbabwe.

A VAST AND VARIED LANDSCAPE

Southern Africa contains deserts, mountains, seashores, grasslands, and forests. Each region has a different kind of climate, a different kind of soil, different plants and animals, and different natural resources.

Below: Bushman's grass grows on the arid plains of southern Africa.

Coasts and Mountains

South Africa is surrounded on three sides by the ocean. The southern and southeastern shores are tropical— warm and rainy. The Drakensberg Mountains lie along the southeastern coastline, facing the sandy beaches of the Indian Ocean.

Left: South Africa has 1,739 miles (2,798 kilometers) of coastline. The Cape of Good Hope, at the southwestern tip of the country, has some beautiful beaches.

Above: Antelopes run through the marshy ground of the Okavango Swamp in Botswana.

Dry Lands

The land west of the Drakensberg Mountains is semiarid—dry with only light rainfall. Farther west, in the Kalahari Desert, the land is flatter and much drier. In much of the desert, grasses and succulents are the only plants that can survive. Succulents are plants such as cacti. They survive by storing water inside their trunks, branches, and leaves. The northern edge of the Kalahari does not look like desert at all. The land is swampy, filled with reeds and other water plants. It is the site of the Okavango Swamp, a vast marshland.

Another Desert

West of the Kalahari is the Namib Desert. This dry region receives almost no rainfall. The thorn bushes that grow here depend on the

morning fog for moisture. Some of the biggest diamond deposits in the world are located underneath the dry sand.

A SWAMP IN THE SAND

The Okavango Swamp changes with the seasons. During the dry season in southern Africa, the swamp dries up. During the rainy season, the swamp fills with water. Flowers bloom (*above left*), and the land becomes green. Some San live near the Okavango Swamp. They are called River Bushmen.

THE KALAHARI

The Kalahari is a vast desert covering approximately 360,000 square miles (932,000 square kilometers). It covers most of Botswana, about one-third of Namibia, and a small part of South Africa. In the desert's southern areas, rainfall is very light—only 5 inches (12.7 centimeters) or less each year. More rain falls in the north and east—as much as 20 inches (50.8 centimeters) annually. But the rainy season lasts only three months per year: December, January, and February.

Hot and Cold

In summer, daytime temperatures in the Kalahari can reach over 100 degrees Fahrenheit (37.7 degrees Celsius). Some people are surprised to learn that winters can be very cold in the Kalahari. In fact, nighttime temperatures sometimes fall as low as 10 degrees Fahrenheit (-12.2 degrees Celsius) in the winter months of June and July.

Right: A San family climbs a sand dune in the Kalahari Desert in Botswana.

Left: Dutch settlers, arriving in southern Africa in the 1600s, called the Kalahari Desert the Great Thirstland.

A Desert of Grass

Many people think of deserts as endless miles of sand, without any plants. But deserts actually have many kinds of plants. Barbed grasses, thorn bushes, and great baobab trees cover many parts of the Kalahari. Many plants survive the dry season by storing up on water during the rainy season. Grasses survive by spreading many short roots over a large area. This way, the roots absorb as much water as possible. Other plants send roots deep into the soil to gather water from beneath the ground.

Rows of Dunes

The western part of the Kalahari contains long, orderly rows of sand dunes. The spaces between the rows are called valleys or streets. The desert wind blows the dunes into a crescent shape. You might picture them as curled-up giants, asleep with their backs against the blowing wind.

THE ELEPHANT TREE

Baobabs (*right*), called elephant trees, can grow to be 60 feet (18 meters) tall. Their thin bark resembles elephant skin, wrinkly and springy to the touch. If you were to lean against the trunk of a baobab tree, you might think you'd backed into the leg of a big elephant. Baobabs can live to be very old, sometimes even one thousand years old.

PRECIOUS VELDKOS

*V*eld is a Dutch word meaning "field." It refers to the vast, dry grasslands of southern Africa, including some parts of the Kalahari Desert. The word *veldkos,* or "field food," refers to the native plants and animals of the veld. These plants and animals have provided food for the San and other groups. Animals, too, rely on the veldkos for food.

Grasses

Grasses are one of the most important veldkos plants. Zebras, wildebeests, impalas, antelopes, and other animals graze on the roots and blades of these grasses. The grasses are bitter to taste, but not poisonous. Insects, birds, and rodents feast on grass seeds. Many animals and birds use grass to make their nests. Grass also helps keep the loose, sandy soil of the Kalahari from blowing away in the wind.

Left: The bright yellow flowers of the quiver tree

Gathering Veldkos Plants

The veld is alive with edible plants—about two hundred species in all. They include melons, olives, figs, nuts, and berries. Artichokes, leeks, truffles (similar to mushrooms), and wild turnips also grow on the veld. People who gather wild plants must know which ones are safe to eat and where to look for them.

Above: Many types of veldkos, including tsama melons, grow in the Kalahari Desert.

QUIVER TREES

Lush green quiver trees (*left*) thrive in the driest regions of southern Africa. Quiver trees, also called *kokerboom,* are not really trees at all. They are actually big plants that sometimes grow to be 30 feet (9.1 meters) high. In winter, quiver trees bloom with bright yellow flowers. To survive droughts (periods without rainfall) quiver trees store water inside their trunks and branches. Quiver wood is sturdy, light, and soft in the center. In earlier times, San hunters hollowed out the branches and shaped them into quivers—containers for arrows.

HUNTERS OF AFRICA

In Africa, animals must hunt to survive. Lions, cheetahs, leopards, and other meat-eaters hunt and kill slower and weaker animals. Even animals that do not eat meat, such as rhinoceroses and giraffes, must be hunters, too. To survive, they must hunt for grasses, leaves, insects, and grubs. In dry regions, especially the central Kalahari, all animals must hunt for water.

With and without Water

In the desert, spotting an animal such as a zebra, leopard, baboon, or hippopotamus is a good clue that drinking water is nearby. These animals need plenty of water to survive, and they know where to look for it. Antelopes can survive with less water. That's because they have extra chambers in their stomachs for storing food and water. These chambers help antelopes survive long periods between meals. Antelopes also digest their food very slowly, drawing out every bit of liquid the food contains.

Keeping Cool

Many desert animals are specially suited to hot, dry weather. The gemsbok, a kind of antelope, has a network of tiny veins that act like a built-in air-conditioning system. Frogs, lizards, tortoises, and mice survive the dry season by estivating. Their breathing, heartbeat, and other body systems slow down. They go into an inactive state similar to sleep. Because their bodies are inactive, the animals don't need much water to survive. Other small animals dig tunnels or burrows beneath the sand to avoid the hot desert sun.

Above: A beautiful gemsbok keeps cool in a water hole in the Kalahari Desert .

No One Is Spared

No animal is too small to be hunted. Large animals often hunt for smaller ones, such as frogs, tortoises, anteaters, porcupines, rabbits, and birds. Some San still hunt these animals, too. They also eat birds' eggs, ants' eggs, bee larvae, locusts, caterpillars, and termites.

Left: A herd of greater kudu, a kind of antelope, drinks at a water hole in the Etosha National Park in Namibia.

THE KALAHARI LION

The Kalahari lion is the undisputed king of the desert. It hunts at night to stay cool and save energy. It kills mostly large animals, like impalas and zebras. But game is scarce, and the lion doesn't find such large animals often. The early San observed lions and other wild animals. They learned some of their hunting techniques by imitating these animals.

ANCIENT WAYS

The San have lived in southern Africa for at least 30,000 years. The early San were hunter-gatherers. They gathered food from the plants and trees that grew around them. Using weapons such as spears and arrows, they also hunted animals for food.

Different Groups

As they hunted and gathered, different groups of San traveled great distances. Each group gradually developed its own words, pronunciations, and traditions. The groups were different, but they were all still part of the San culture. Two of the largest groups were the G/wi and the !Kung, both of which still live in southern Africa.

Right: A Kalahari San makes a fire by blowing on hot coals and grass.

Master Hunters

San hunters developed deadly poison arrows, used for killing large animals. The arrows were made of bone and flint, a kind of rock. When an animal was shot with a poison arrow, the poison irritated its flesh. The animal rubbed the wound, spreading the poison into its nervous system. The poison then killed the animal.

Above: This ancient stone tool was used for chopping. The surfaces have sharp edges.

Chemists of the Kalahari

The Kalahari San used chemicals from plants, reptiles, and insects to make their poisons. They knew exactly how much poison was needed to kill an animal without contaminating its meat. One kind of poison comes from the larvae of the chrysomelid beetle. The beetle's larva lies in a hard, tube-shaped cocoon. When a San hunter prepared an arrow, he rolled the cocoon between his fingers, crushing the larva inside without cracking the cocoon shell. Then he made a tiny hole in one end of the shell and neatly squeezed the crushed larva onto the arrowhead. Some San still prepare poison arrows in this way.

Above: San arrows are small but deadly because of the poison used to coat the tips.

OTHER ANCIENT PEOPLES

The Khoi, another group of native people, live in many of the same areas as the San. They are similar to the San in appearance and language. While the early San lived mostly by hunting and gathering, the early Khoi lived chiefly by herding cattle and sheep. Despite big differences between these two cultures, people sometimes call them by one combined name, Khoisan.

THE ARRIVAL OF OUTSIDERS

Europeans saw Africa as a vast, open place with plenty of space and animals for everyone. They began to explore the west coast of Africa in the 1400s. Later, they formed settlements in parts of Africa, including southern Africa where the San lived. The settlers built fences, roads, and farms. The San had never built permanent homes or cities, so the European settlers did not recognize them as landowners, with rights to the territory. The settlers did not understand the San's traditions. The San were just as puzzled by the ways of the settlers.

Left and below: Illustrations of European ships that sailed to Africa in the 1500s

Explorers and Immigrants

In 1652, Jan van Riebeeck and about seventy-five other Dutch settlers founded a colony at the Cape of Good Hope, at the southwestern tip of Africa. The settlers called themselves Afrikaners. They created a large farm to supply goods to European sailors rounding the cape on the way to and from India. Eventually, some farmers left the colony to start smaller farms nearby. These farmers were called trek Boers, or "traveling farmers." The Boers built their farms anywhere they liked. They took over San hunting and gathering lands. As more and more Boers arrived, the San gradually moved away from Africa's southern coasts, toward the desert lands to the north.

The British and the Bantu

In the late 1700s, British troops arrived in the Cape colony. They clashed with the Afrikaners in a number of bloody battles. The peaceable San wanted no part of the fighting. But many of them were killed in the wars between the British and the Afrikaners. Meanwhile, another group of African people, the Bantu, had traveled into San territory from the north. The Bantu began taking over San territory. Crowded from the north and south, some San moved deeper and deeper into the desert.

HUNTERS AND POACHERS

European explorers spread stories of exotic African elephants, lions, and rhinoceroses. Adventurers from around the world came to track, hunt, and kill the animals. Some liked the excitement of the hunt. Others wanted to collect decorative animal skins, trophy heads, or prized tusks. A few trappers shipped living animals across the ocean to faraway zoos and carnivals. In modern times, hunting is strictly regulated in Africa. But many people hunt wild animals illegally. Illegal hunting is called poaching, and people who hunt illegally are called poachers.

CONFLICT AND CONQUEST

The San did not have a system of government. They chose no group leaders or rulers. In more than 30,000 years of history, the San never began a war or fought battles among themselves. With this record of peacefulness, it is easy to understand why the San wanted no part of the fighting with European or other native groups in southern Africa.

Below: Boer soldiers in southern Africa during the late 1800s

Pushed Aside by Fighting

In the 1800s, the British, Afrikaners, and Bantus fought one another for control of territory in South Africa, including valuable diamond and gold mines. Occasionally, the Portuguese, French, and Germans also tried to gain control of the land. As outside rulers claimed new territory, they created new laws and new borders. The San saw only mountains and oceans as boundaries. They did not understand the new borders, or the fighting and bloodshed. As the Europeans and Bantu tribes took over more territory, the San were either killed or pushed into the wilderness. Some San retreated to the harsh terrain of the Kalahari Desert—lands that no one else wanted.

Above: Three Boer soldiers pose for a photograph in the early 1900s.

Giving Up the Old Ways

The European newcomers brought many changes to San life. They brought deadly diseases, such as smallpox, that the San had never known before. Many San died of these diseases. The San population began to decline. Many San abandoned their traditional lifestyle. Some of them took jobs on the farms of settlers who had taken over their hunting and gathering grounds.

FORCED INTO SLAVERY

From the 1700s through to the early 1900s, both European settlers and other native black tribes kidnapped San children and used them as slaves. Because they were clever and gentle, the children quickly learned to serve as household servants or skillful farmworkers. Others worked as game trackers. In 1814 and 1833, the British government passed antislavery laws that were supposed to stop this practice. But the laws were not always enforced. San parents sometimes fought back when their children were kidnapped. But with their simple weapons, they were no match for Europeans armed with guns.

SEPARATED BY RACE

*A*partheid is a Dutch word that means "separateness." It refers to the practice of separating people by race. Between 1948 and 1991, the South African government enforced a series of apartheid laws. Under these laws, people in South Africa were separated into four groups: black, white, Asian, and colored (mixed race). People of different races were not allowed to mix with each other. Black people had few rights. In many places, black people were forced to live in separate towns and settlements. They lived there in poverty, cut off from the rest of South Africa. The lives of Asian and mixed-race people were also restricted, but black people received the harshest treatment under apartheid.

The San under Apartheid

The apartheid laws further divided black people into ten major subgroups. From 1951 to 1991, all South Africans had to register with the government according to race and subgroup. But with their unique appearance, the San did not fit into any of the subgroups. Many San did not register. They remained in isolated areas, living as hunter-gatherers without government interference. Other San suffered under apartheid. Many were forced off their land by both white and black farmers. They ended up in poverty in government camps.

Apartheid's End

Apartheid laws were gradually repealed in South Africa and ended in the early 1990s. Afterward, the South African government tried to compensate native groups for the wrongs they had endured during the apartheid years. In some places, lands that had been taken over by farmers were returned to native people. Some lands were set aside for the San. But, in several instances, the San found that other native groups claimed the same land as their own.

Above and opposite: These soldiers were part of the Omega Battalion, the largest group of San soldiers fighting in the South African army in the 1970s.

FORCED RELOCATION

In the 1970s, many San from Namibia were forced to fight in the South African army against Namibian rebels. Namibia was at that time occupied by South Africa. After the fighting was over, the San were afraid to return to their homes in Namibia. They thought that the former rebels there might strike back at them. They gave up their lives as hunter-gatherers and moved to crude camps built by the South African government. There, they had no way to learn a living.

In Botswana in the 1980s and 1990s, thousands of San were forced from their homes in the Central Kalahari Game Reserve. They were moved into bleak camps, where they were dependent on government handouts. The Botswana government wanted the San removed from the reserve so it could develop tourism and valuable diamond mines there.

INTO THE MODERN WORLD

It is hard for the San to maintain their traditional ways in the modern world. They can no longer hunt freely as their ancestors did. In many parts of southern Africa, hunting has been outlawed or severely restricted. In addition, wildlife populations have declined—many animals have been killed illegally, or moved to zoos or game preserves. As more land is taken over for roads, cities, and buildings, there are fewer places for the San to look for wild foods. Because their ancient lifestyle has changed, some modern San work as farm laborers. A few work at wildlife parks. Many other San are unemployed. They often live in government camps, in poor conditions without good medical care.

Below: A San farmworker tends lambs in South Africa.

San Sheepshearers

Some San live south of the Kalahari, in a region of South Africa called the Karoo. Along with many Bantu, Khoi, and Afrikaner people, these San work as farm laborers, usually sheepshearers. They shear wool with hand-operated clippers, which do not damage wool or hurt sheep the way electric clippers sometimes do.

Above: A San gamekeeper in Nambia's Etosha National Park.

The Promise of Ecotourism

In the future, the San might benefit from a new idea called ecotourism. This is the practice of visiting natural areas without disturbing them—with the utmost respect for the land, plants, and animals. The San know a lot about animal habits, natural foods, and herbal medicines. The San might be able to earn money by teaching tourists about their ancient traditions.

FROM TRACKING TO CYBER-TRACKING

The early San hunters were expert trackers. They were skilled at searching out animal tracks and following game through the wilderness. In modern times, some San (*left*) work at wildlife parks. There, they track animals in a different way. They keep track of the animals' feeding, migration, and mating habits. This information helps scientists learn more about wild animals and how to protect them. A new palm-size computer called the Cyber Tracker helps San park workers keep records and send data to park rangers and researchers.

GOLDEN FACES

With their small size and golden skin tones, the San look quite different from neighboring African peoples. Some historians think they might be related to the Bantus, but the Bantus are much darker, taller, and larger than the San. Other historians believe that the San might be related to the original people of ancient Egypt, who lived far to the north of San territory. But questions about the San's heritage remain a mystery.

Appearance

The average San adult male is about 5 feet (1.5 meters) tall. San women are slightly shorter. Both men and women have delicate hands and feet, prominent foreheads, flat noses, and high cheekbones. Their faces are heart-shaped, and their ears are tiny with very small lobes. Their hair grows naturally in small tufts, and they usually wear it very short. While the sun tans their skin darker, its natural color is yellowgolden to apricot, and it develops distinctive foldlike wrinkles as they age.

Left: A San man wears a cloak to keep warm.

Clothing: Old and New

Many modern San prefer to dress as their ancestors did. They wear animal skins tied around their waists like aprons. Sometimes a woman wears a shawl called a *kaross,* usually made from antelope skin. Karosses are also used as slings for carrying babies or food. Other modern-day San wear Western-style clothing, much like clothes worn in Europe and the United States.

Larger Than Life

The San may be short compared to Europeans and Americans, but they have never seen themselves that way. Centuries-old San rock paintings show the San, the Bantu, and European settlers at work and play. In all the paintings, the San are pictured to be just as tall as the Europeans, the Bantus, and even mighty Zulu warriors, who were known for their great size.

Above: San children in Johannesburg, South Africa, pose for a photograph.

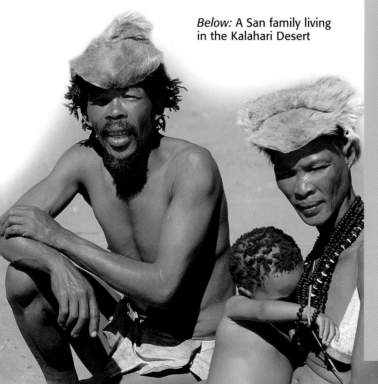

Below: A San family living in the Kalahari Desert

THE CHANGING FACE OF THE SAN

Modern San people are not always easy to spot. That's because they live in small groups scattered across six different countries. Many dress in modern clothing and speak English and Afrikaans, a South African language. And their faces and bodies have changed since ancient times. Modern San eat a more balanced diet than their hunter-gatherer ancestors ate. With better nutrition, each generation grows a little taller. What's more, if a San marries a European, Afrikaner, or Bantu, the couple's children will be racially mixed. They won't look distinctively San.

SAN HOMES

The early San were always on the move, looking for new hunting grounds and food sources. It didn't make sense for them to build permanent homes. Instead, they built simple, temporary shelters out of grass and sticks. When San moved camp, they simply built new shelters in a new spot.

Traditional Homes

Some San shelters had walls but not roofs. Called windbreaks, these simple structures provided protection from only the wind. In cold weather, people built fires inside windbreaks. In rainy weather, people covered them with roofs and waterproofed them with a coating of glue made from animal skins. Groups worked together to build the shelters. Men gathered sticks to make a frame. Women wove grasses around the frame to makes walls. Most San homes were very tiny, only about 3 feet (0.9 meters) tall and 4 feet (1.2 meters) wide. They provided shelter for just one family—usually the parents and an only child.

Left: A San woman mends a hut made of grass and sticks.

Above: A San village in Botswana. The Botswana government is trying to relocate San to permanent villages such as this one.

Modern Homes

Kalahari San still live in traditional windbreaks. Other modern San live in simple, handmade huts. Yet other San live in tents or buildings provided by the government. The buildings are usually basic wooden structures, with earthen floors and no electricity or plumbing. Only a small number of San live in comfortable, modern housing with electric power and running water.

PEOPLE OF THE CART

Some San (*left*) live a modern version of the hunter-gatherer's traveling lifestyle. Called "people of the cart," or *karretjiemense,* these San live in donkey-drawn wooden carts, stocked with all their possessions, including blankets and cooking utensils. They travel from farm to farm to find jobs, often working as sheepshearers. Sometimes they gather plants and roots for extra food. Karretjiemense children attend schools near the farms where their parents work.

CLANS AND COMMUNITY LIFE

San people live in small groups called clans. The typical clan has about thirty members, although some have as few as four or five people. Usually, everyone in the clan is related. People switch clans by marrying into a new family. Sometimes, people who are unhappy with their clan leave to join another.

The Rules of Sharing

The early San had no money system and did very little trading. They survived by gathering, hunting, and sharing with other members of the clan. When a hunter brought home his kill, he and his family took the largest and best portions, such as the neck and shoulders of the animal. But, according to need, other families in the clan took a portion of the kill, too.

Below: San children play in their village in Botswana.

A Traveling Lifestyle

San hunter-gatherers were always on the move, looking for new food supplies. They stayed in one main area, rotating locations about every three weeks. When all the plants and animals in one spot were depleted, the San left for a new location. They rotated back to earlier spots when food supplies there had been replenished—when new plants had grown and animals had returned.

Left: This bird, the heuning wyser, helps the San find honey. When the bird finds a beehive, it flutters around, trying to get the bee larvae inside. The San follow the bird to the hive and break open a part of the hive. The San love the honey inside, and the bird gets the bee larvae.

Make Your Own Decisions

In a San clan, everyone is allowed to make his or her own decisions, and each person tries to make choices that don't offend anyone else. If there are conflicts within the clan, the San settle them by telling comic stories that make the people involved laugh. For the San, laughter helps people set aside their anger and unhappiness.

CHILD'S PLAY

Like all children, San children (*right*) enjoy playing games. They use melons to play ball. Boys sometimes pretend to be hunters. They carve soft wood or roots into tiny bows and arrows—but without the poison tips. Girls play with dolls carved from wood or roots. They also play "mother" to the younger children in the clan, which gives them important practice for adult life. San children did not attend school in earlier eras, but modern San children usually attend school for part of the year.

WOMEN— THE GATHERERS

I n earlier eras, hunting and gathering were the two jobs that allowed the San to survive. These activities provided the San with all of the food they needed. The San divided these two jobs between the sexes: women gathered and men hunted.

Gathering Food

San women can often spot edible plants from a great distance. They can also find food in areas that at first appear to have no plants. For instance, a thin crack across the dirt tells San gatherers that a truffle might be buried below. A tiny withered leaf might indicate an edible root underneath the dry soil. Women dig at the soil with sharp sticks, uncovering roots and vegetables to use as food and medicines. They use karosses as slings for carrying the provisions home. When full of veldkos, a kaross might weigh as much as 30 pounds (13.6 kilograms).

Left: San women often go out in groups to gather food.

Minding the Children

Who looks after the children while their mothers are out gathering food? Sometimes, elderly men and women are the baby-sitters. As the elder people supervise, they also share their skills and wisdom with the children. Sometimes, mothers carry their babies in slings on their backs when they go out gathering food.

Above: Some San still eat a diet of nuts, berries, and edible larvae.

Unusual Pots and Pans

Traditionally, most San made dishes and bowls out of empty melons, tortoiseshells, and ostrich eggshells. They carved cooking tools from animal bone. A small group of San in Botswana made pottery from hardened mud and clay. Modern San usually use modern containers such as clay pottery, cast-iron cookware, wooden bowls, and enamelware.

USEFUL OSTRICH EGGS

The San love eating scrambled ostrich eggs, but they value the eggshell as much as the food inside. Ostrich eggs are very large—up to 7 inches (17.8 centimeters) long and 5 inches (12.7 centimeters) wide. The San carve decorative patterns into big pieces of shell, which they use as bowls, cups, and ladles. They also use whole shells as water containers. First they pierce the shells with a sharpened piece of bone and drain out the egg white and yolk. Then, using a reed, they drip water into the empty shells (*right*). They plug the holes with grass and bury the eggshells along desert pathways. On future hunting trips, hunters can then locate the shells, which hold valuable water.

MEN—THE HUNTERS

San men were skilled hunters. But they believed that a hunter should not become too proud or make others jealous of his success. If a San hunter made several kills in a row, he would hunt less frequently, giving other hunters a chance to kill more animals.

Following in the Footsteps

San men hunted in twos or threes. They took quick and quiet steps as they tracked their game, walking in the footprints of the man ahead of them. While hunting, they communicated with each other by making soft noises that resembled birdcalls.

Below: Stalking game required much patience and silence.

Tricking the Hippopotamus

Hippopotamus meat was a favorite San dish. To hunt a hippo, the San dug large pits near rivers. They lined the pits with spears and covered the pits with vegetation. The hunters then teased a hippo until it charged them. They led the charging animal toward the hidden pit. The hippo was usually killed when it fell on the spears hidden inside the pit.

Above: Hippopotamuses swim in the Okavango River in Botswana.

Tools for Hunting and Fishing

In addition to spears, San hunters used clubs, bows, and their deadly poison-tipped arrows. They made snares to catch small birds. They also used sticky glues from plants and trees to catch birds and other small animals. The River Bushmen of the Okavango Swamp fished from canoes. They used aloe plants to make fishing nets and baskets. They also wove baskets out of grass.

HUNTING PARTNERS

Hunters often use dogs as partners, but imagine using a lion as a hunting partner! San hunters did just that. They covered their bodies with a foul-smelling paste made from plants and roots. Lions would not attack the hunters because of the bad smell. Then, as a lion stalked its own game, the hunters patiently followed. They waited as the lion killed and ate its prey. While the lion ate, the San built a fire. After a time, the smoke and flames bothered the lion and drove it away. When the lion left, the San took the remaining meat.

UNIQUE LANGUAGES

Originally, the San didn't have a written language. Their tales and lessons were passed down orally—by word of mouth. Later, after Europeans arrived in Africa, San words were written down using the English-language and other alphabets.

Lost Wisdom

Different San groups developed languages that were similar, but had slight differences in grammar, pronunciation, and spelling. Most of these languages have never been taught in any school. In fact, most modern San children grow up without ever hearing or speaking their own language, or seeing it in print. Most modern San speak English and Afrikaans, the language of the Dutch and other early white settlers in Africa. In some places, only a few elders still know the San languages. As these elders die, the languages are lost with them. As the San languages die out, the San's knowledge of their history, culture, and legends also vanishes, along with their vast knowledge about plants, animals, and the environment.

Below: An outdoor school for San children in the 1970s

Above: A San clan enjoys an afternoon chat.

Clicks and Pops

The languages of the San and Khoi peoples together are called Khoisan languages. They can be hard for outsiders to learn. These languages have more sounds than most other languages, including distinctive clicking and popping sounds. There are no letters in the English-language alphabet to match the Khoisan clicks and pops. So when people write words that include these sounds, they use special symbols such as ≠, //, and ! The clicks and pops are unfamiliar to people who speak European, Asian, or some other African languages. The only sound in English that resembles a Khoisan click is the "tsk tsk" sound that people sometimes make to show disapproval.

Listening to Nature

The San believe that animals can talk to people and to each other. San hunters could expertly imitate the calls of animals, and they paid careful attention to the sounds of nature, such as rain and wind. Many non-San people say that the San languages sound like the soft crackling and rustling of the desert wind and sand.

CLICK, CLICK, CLICK

To feel what it's like to speak San, press your tongue against the roof of your mouth and make a clicking sound. Then move your tongue to another place in your mouth and click again. Keep moving your tongue around, making as many different clicking sounds as you can.

TIME FOR ART

Above: An ostrich egg decorated by a San artist

Historians once thought that the early San were concerned only with survival in the harsh African environment. But San legends and art tell a different story. In fact, the San enjoyed music, dancing, storytelling, and painting. They worked hard to gather what they needed from the earth, but they also took time to enjoy themselves with family and friends.

Skilled Craftspeople

The early San were skilled craftspeople. They made tools out of animal bones, wood, and pieces of metal. They decorated tools with carvings and beads. One unusual hunting tool was an ostrich costume stretched over a wooden frame. The costume included a real ostrich's head and neck, with ostrich feathers covering the rest of the frame. Wearing this costume, San hunters made ostrich sounds and imitated the bird's movements. Wild animals were fooled by the disguise, and they allowed the hunters to approach them. Once the hunters got close, the animals were easily killed.

Right: A San child plays with a lamellaphone, or finger piano.

Clever Musicians

The San also crafted musical instruments. They filled dried butterfly cocoons with tiny pieces of ostrich eggshell to make rattles. They lined hundreds of rattles end-to-end on a leather strip, creating 5-foot (1.5-meter) chains. Dancers wrapped one chain around each ankle. The rattle chains were made so well that some dancers wore the same pair for a whole lifetime. The San also used reeds to make single and double flutes. They used leather and a stone to make an instrument that rang like a bell. They also made many types of drums using animal hides stretched over frames.

Songs of the San

The San liked to make music while they played and relaxed. They also sang, whistled, and tapped out rhythms as they prepared animal hides, made tools, and performed other tasks. Some songs told stories of daily life or ancient legends. Other songs were part of important religious ceremonies. Yet others were nonsense songs sung just for fun.

Right: A San man plays a stringed instrument using a wooden bow.

TORTOISESHELL ORCHESTRA

Using the shells of large mountain tortoises, the San made stringed instruments that resembled cellos. They used tightly stretched antelope tendons to make the strings. They used the shells of smaller tortoises to make smaller stringed instruments, similar to modern-day violins and mandolins.

THE RHYTHM OF LIFE

Dancing was a part of daily San life. As soon as babies learned to walk, their parents and older siblings taught them difficult dance steps. Many dances imitated the movements of animals. San storytellers often told tales and legends while other people danced. People also danced to make their work more enjoyable. Important dances were at the center of religious ceremonies and celebrations.

Below: A San baby dances as her older relatives create rhythm by clapping.

All Night Long

At the end of a day of hunting or gathering, nightfall brought relief from the desert heat. It was also a time to celebrate and dance under the twinkling stars. Dancing together around a community fire brought clan members closer to each other and closer to the spirits of nature. The San often danced and sang until dawn.

Above: A group of San sing while a boy performs a traditional dance.

Telling Stories

San storytellers were highly respected. Some stories were the property of everyone—any person could tell them. Other stories were "owned" by one person. No one could tell these stories without the owner's permission. Because the early San did not have a written language, storytelling helped them pass down accounts of their history from one generation to the next.

BABOON AND ZEBRA

An old San story says that the baboon was stingy. He would not share his water with the zebra (*right*). The two animals argued, and the zebra became so angry that he kicked the baboon very hard. The baboon landed on the ground with such a smack that his rump became bare. But the zebra stumbled from his own forceful kick and fell into the fire, leaving his fur permanently scorched with black stripes. This story explains why baboons have bare bottoms and zebras have black stripes.

PAINTING ON ROCK

Some early San were talented artists who painted or etched (carved) pictures on rock walls. In fact, thousands of beautiful San paintings can still be seen on large rocks and cave walls in southern Africa. These walls are like open-air rock art galleries.

Right: A San artist at work in a village in South Africa

The Best Artists

Art historians think that the San permitted only their best artists to make paintings and etchings. These skilled artists were famous among the San. They traveled between clans and were treated as honored guests. Many artists were also shamans—people who could tell the future, heal the sick, and communicate with spirits. Their paintings showed events from the real world as well as images from the spirit world.

Paints and Brushes from Nature

San artists used quills, feathers, sticks, bones, and even their own fingers as paintbrushes. A sharpened animal bone was good for painting a thin line, while a frayed stick made a thick brushstroke. To make paints, the San crushed colored rocks and other natural items into powders, then mixed them with egg white, water, or animal blood. Iron oxide produced red paint. White paint came from silica, white clay, or bird droppings. Charcoal, soot, and manganese were used to make black paint.

Above: The Twyfelfontein Caves in Namibia have many beauiful examples of San rock art.

Rock Wall Galleries

More than 2,500 San etchings and paintings can be seen on large rock walls at Twyfelfontein in Namibia. These artworks are many centuries old. Several thousand more San paintings have been found at Tsodilo Hills in Botswana. These pictures show scenes of dancing, hunting, shamans, and animals, carefully painted in shades of yellow and red. Other important rock art sites are located in Lesotho and South Africa.

WHAT THE SAN PAINTED

San rock art (*right*) tells history through pictures. Ancient San artists painted scenes of hunting, gathering, and dancing. Animals were painted with realistic detail. Some paintings show spirits that are half-human, half-animal. Other paintings show frightening creatures with fire for eyes and enormous horns. San art also tells the story of the arrival of the Europeans and the Bantu. It shows farmlands, horses, and battles.

SAN BELIEFS

The San believe in one highest spirit, the Great God, who looks after all living creatures. The Great God is said to live in the eastern sky with the rising sun. He is invisible to people, but they can feel his presence in the darkness and quiet of the night. The San also believe in animal spirits. Elands, a kind of antelope, are thought to be special messengers from the spirit world.

Below: A San healer examines a patient.

Left: A San healer treats a patient during a ceremony, while women chant and clap their hands.

Healing Powers

The San often perform healing ceremonies to help sick people. During the ceremonies, people dance to receive healing powers from the spirit world. Many dances imitate the movements of animals. The Eland Dance is thought to bring healing to the feet. The Giraffe Dance brings healing to the head.

Left: San dances are sometimes named for animals such as giraffes.

Death Rites

After a San person dies, some groups coat the body with animal fat and a red powder before burial. This mixture mummifies, or preserves, the body. The San usually bury people in a curled-up position, sitting upright. Traditionally, the San buried a dead man along with the weapons he used when he was alive.

HELPFUL MANTIS

Mantis is the name of a San god. He takes the form of a praying mantis (*left*). Mantis, like the eland, is also thought to be a messenger of the gods. He sometimes brings bad luck and misfortune. But he can also be helpful. The San say that Mantis first gave them fire.

CELEBRATIONS OF LIFE

The early San did not observe holidays on specific dates like people in Western cultures do. Instead, the San celebrated events of daily life as they happened. For example, the San celebrated when a child became a young adult, when much-needed rains fell, or when a hunt was successful.

Below: A San community celebrates the coming-of-age of a San girl during the Gemsbok Ceremony.

The Gemsbok Ceremony

The entire San community celebrated when a San girl became a young woman— usually around age thirteen. The clan built a special hut for the celebration. The girl went inside the hut and could have only female visitors. Every night, the women of the clan danced around the hut, chanting and imitating the movements of the gemsbok, considered the most beautiful of all animals. On the final night, the men joined in the dance. The young woman was then presented to the rest of clan as a young adult.

Above: Gemsboks graze in a South African nature reserve.

The Eland Ceremony

When a boy was strong enough to handle a bow and arrow, usually about age fourteen, he was sent to kill an eland. When he returned to the clan with his kill, he stayed in his hut and avoided all women. The clan cooked the eland on a special fire, separate from all other food. The boy did not eat his first kill, but the rest of the clan feasted on the meat. Before the clan recognized the boy as truly a man, he had to kill both a male and a female eland.

CELEBRATING THE KILL

Hunters sometimes returned to the clan with news of a large kill, too big to transport. When that happened, the entire clan went to the kill site. The meat was prepared, cooked, and eaten right there. A celebration began soon afterward. Women clapped their hands, and men stamped their feet. The celebration was held to thank the spirit of the animal for the nourishment it had provided.

GLOSSARY

apartheid: a policy of racial segregation, enforced by the South African government between 1948 and 1991

climate: the typical weather found in a certain region

depleted: used up

ecotourism: travel practices that involve touring wild areas without damaging the natural environment

estivating: surviving a hot, dry period by going into a dormant state, similar to sleep

hunter-gatherers: people who survive by hunting game and gathering wild plants for food

kaross (kah-RAWS): a shawl. San women also use karosses to collect veldkos.

lamellaphone: a finger piano made from a wooden board with thin metal strips nailed to it

larva: an animal in its immature form. Insect larvae are generally wingless and wormlike.

migration: the movement of animals from one place to another. Animals generally migrate to find new food sources or breeding grounds.

repealed: removed or formally ended

semiarid region: a dry place that receives only light rainfall

shamans: people who can tell the future, heal the sick, and communicate with the spirit world

succulent: a plant that stores moisture in its stem or leaves

tendons: tough body tissue that connects muscle to bone

tracking: quietly and patiently following an animal without being heard or seen by it

tropical region: a place that is hot and rainy year-round

veld: open country, bearing grass, bushes, and shrubs, found in parts of southern Africa

Western cultures: Western Europe, the United States, and other industrialized, democratic cultures

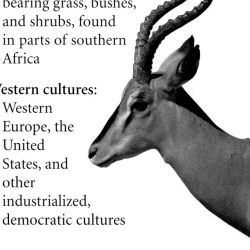

FINDING OUT MORE

Books

Canesso, Claudio. *South Africa*. Philadelphia: Chelsea House Publishers, 1999.

Lauard, Nicholas. *The Wildlife Parks of Africa*. Salem, NH: Salem House, 1986.

Lauré, Jason. *Namibia*. Chicago: Children's Press, 1993.

Omer-Cooper, J. D. *History of Southern Africa*. Portsmouth, NH: James Currey, Ltd. and Heinemann Educational Books, Inc., 1987.

Owens, Delia, and Mark Owens. *The Eye of the Elephant: An Epic Adventure in the African Wilderness.* Boston, New York, and London: Houghton Mifflin Company, 1992.

Ross, Karen. *Okavango: Jewel of the Kalahari*. London: BBC Books, 1987.

Videos

Cry of the Kalahari. Books on Tape, 1988.

Night Creatures of the Kalahari. NOVA, 1989.

Okavango: Africa's Wild Oasis. National Geographic, 1996.

Websites

<http://www.afroventures.com/maps/central kalahari.htm>

<http://www.museums.org.za/sam/resource/arch/khoisan.htm>

<http://www.national geographic.com/ngm/0102>

Organizations

Kalahari Peoples Fund
P.O. Box 7855, University Station
Austin, Texas 78713-7855
Tel: (512) 453-8935
Website: <http://www.kalaharipeoples.org>

Rock Art Institute
Department of Archaeology
Van Riet Lowe Building
University of the Witwatersrand
P. Bag 3
P.O. Wits 2050
Johannesburg, South Africa
Tel: (27) 11 717-6056

Survival
6 Charterhouse Buildings
London EC1M 7ET, United Kingdom
Tel: (44) 207-687-8700
E-mail: <info@survival-international.org>
Website: <http:/www.survival.org.uk>

INDEX

ABOUT THE AUTHOR

Linda J. Parker is an author, educator, and researcher whose works include both fiction and nonfiction for adults and young readers. She is a magna cum laude graduate of the University of Kentucky. In 1999, she left her career as a corporate vice president to write full-time. She was introduced to San history and culture while she was studying their beautiful rock paintings. She credits her mother for her love of learning and her father for her determination. To both of them she is forever grateful.

PICTURE CREDITS

(B=bottom; C=center; F= far; I=inset; L=left; M=main; R=right; T=top)

Camera Press: 18M, 28B • Carla Signori Jones/Images of Africa Photobank: 12M, 33TR, 46BR • Darrel C. H. Plowes: 3BR, 6B, 9I, 10L, 15TL, 15CR, 24BL, 27T, 37BR, 41B, 43B, 45T, • Dave G. Houser/Houserstock: 43CL • David Keith Jones/Images of Africa Photobank: 7T, 7BI, 11TR, 13T, 39BR • Friedrich von Hörsten/Images of Africa Photobank: 1, 5BI, 8-9M, 22M, 25BL, 27B • Jason Lauré: 20-21, 23BI, 25TR, 29BR, 30BL, 32-33M, 36TL, 36-37, 40 • John Hone: cover • Lanz von Hörsten/Images of Africa Photobank: 6CL • Northwind Picture Archives: 16CL, 16BR • Peter Ginn: 14M, 29TL, 35T, 39T • Sonia Halliday Photography: 4-5M, 23TR, 26BL, 31BR, 34B, 38B, 43T, 44-45M • Topham Picturepoint: 17TR, 19T • Trip Photographic Library: 9T, 17BL, 31-32T, 41T, 42 • Vanessa Burger/Images of Africa Photobank: 2T, 11M